NIGHT SONG

Andrés Rodríguez

TIA CHUCHA PRESS
CHICAGO

*Acknowledgments are made to the following publications
in which some of the poems in this book first appeared:*

THE BILINGUAL REVIEW: "Papa Cayo," "Summer"

LOVE IN MANY TUNES: "Wound"

NEW CHICANA/CHICANO WRITING, edited by Charles Tatum
and published by the University of Arizona Press:
"Banners," "Fire and Water," "To My Mother"

QUARRY WEST : "Banners"

WILDERNESS: "The Earth"

ECOS: A different version of "For a Kickapoo Girl"

Back cover photo: Joseph Parker
Book design: Jane Brunette Kremsreiter

Printed in the United States

ISBN 1-882688-05-8

Library of Congress Catalog Card Number: 94-60997

TIA CHUCHA PRESS
A Project of the Guild Complex
PO Box 476969
Chicago IL 60647
312-252-5321
Fax: 312-252-5388

*This project is partially supported by grants from the National
Endowment for the Arts, the Illinois Arts Council, and the City
of Chicago, Department of Cultural Affairs. Special thanks to the
Lannan Foundation for a grant to publicize this and other Tía
Chucha Press projects.*

Para La Familia

CONTENTS

The poet or painter steers his life to maim
Himself somehow for the job. His job is Love
Imagined into words or paint to make
An object that will stand and will not move.

—W.S. GRAHAM

YEARS LIKE BROKEN GLASS

ONE

THE SHUTTER

Here is the first, my father age twelve,
standing at the end of a long furrow.
He holds a machete in one hand.
His shoulders bulge like hillocks across
a dark waistcoat, short, threadbare.
The field behind him has already been picked clean.
Silence, a marble grey sky closing in,
complete that boy's long wooden gaze.

Ten years later in a sunlit bivouac,
he stands bare-chested in the brassy air,
a cluster of leaves upended in flight.
He's gazing uncertainly between
the slender stripped trees
at something moving but invisibly.
It must be France, or Germany, or Spain,
a harvest or destroyed field.

The shutter falls and opens
onto a street filled with snow.
Laughing, he changes himself,
becomes the man who's been gone
wherever I looked. And here
he's looking back, the past filled in
with tar papered houses, blurred wings,
the light, the dust, seeking attachments.

FIRE AND WATER

There was a fire once when they lived together
in the old house. He had cleaned the stove
with kerosene, then turned the burner on.
He would have been killed but for something
that loves a fool. My screaming uncle
ran through every room, *Quick, water!*
Grandfather, helpless and gentle in his wheelchair,
laughed at uncle, *¿Pos cómo? ¡No puedo!*
He laughed so hard (he later told me)
that he almost found the strength to walk again.

I can see them now, years later:
Grandfather, ninety, toothless and crippled,
laughing with all his years at uncle,
gaunt and shriveled and wild with cancer,
looking everywhere, nowhere, for water.
Water would have drowned the flames
and what they needed was fire—
fire for old broken railroad bones,
fire for diseased, blackened packinghouse bones.

Sometime later, after uncle had died,
grandfather heard a voice one night
repeating slowly from the withered *milpa*.
A child? His dead wife calling?
He knew better than to answer the sound
of water rushing around the trees.

SUMMER

They are uncalled for in the snowbound yard.
Green apples flood the whitened space
where you drop from a tree of sleep
and forgotten dreams, calling me to follow.
My sister, boxed inside a window,
pulls back from the gauzy curtains and is gone.
My brother, not yet born, sleeps inside
my mother rocking silent on the porch.
It is summer as you call and call.

We fire *piedras* at the *gallos,*
their torn-out feather bodies
leaping by twos at the wire fence,
screaming at our backs till their cries
are inaudible from the lot. We dance
among the shells of torched cars
that sprout weeds man-high and alive.
We move beyond, finding a bucket,
and dip our cupped hands to drink.
And there, before this darkest light,
we taste the water of death in all things.
That's what you, in the pure silence,
mean to me this second time.

I was too young to know what unmade you,
too young to know the story of blood's claim:
you the thirsty monkey, the cousin
dropping from desire's green height.
And now as I sit here, cold, alone,
looking at the yard blanketed with snow,

they are uncalled for: this summer fruit
and year-old news of your death.

With help from you, time invents all things
that wake me to my own dreaming.
We're listening to the *chicharras*
in the middle of a white country road.
The stars cast their fitful light
in your eyes now distinct as glass.
The dark summer wind lifts your hair.
A light from my aunt's house
pours silvery threads into the night,
and you break from my side,
disappearing in a collar of bare trees
interlaced with the stars, brief points,
years I chew like broken glass.

THE KILLING FLOOR

That morning inside the Swift packing house
we went on the killing floor together,
grey smoky light and cold air in winter.
You pointed out meat hooks, crank and conveyor belt,
sick with stoic manhood that weighed on you
like a blood-mark from that frozen room.

Sawdust swept down and powdered your face
as I twitched across an elevated platform.
Stranded below me, you seemed small, childlike,
looking up from the narrow tier abutted
by a tilting rail. I watched you, father,
withdrawing from everything outside you.

The roof shivered like a spine, pinching
the hollow above me as you passed from sight,
a slim moonbeam in the dark below.
A cold draft descended. Something else
floated down, moon-white, filial, silent,
and followed you to the tank house

dragging a carcass skewered with knives.
I called to it. Then it too passed,
the cross-marked fire door closing shut behind,
and the hollow of my voice
deep and knotty over the haunted floor.
I was no longer your fine child

but a bone or mineral in another body.
Throughout that dark place I heard
one door after another swing shut,
and you, moving outside, ask something
swallowed by the chaos of the wind,
then climbed down after the ringing silence
to cross over with you into this life.

ZOOLOGICAL GARDENS

In the aviary pale sunlight glazes an egret's eye
that watches me suck on heavy air of fronds,
the domed house of clacking, wingbeats, feathers and droppings,
a loony bin too much even for us.
They don't look like dinosaurs to me, Chuy says,
so we return to our compulsions.

The big cats stride back and forth across the cage,
breath a visible fire among the rocks and pools.
We're never there at feeding time
but see all sorts of blood and bones,
the savanna's black night cut through with numbing roars
and the antelope's wide flickering eyes.
I like the pit slime and stinking rock moss
where the crocodile whips his dragontail
to kill the English adventurer or native poacher.
Chuy tells me that when a sparrow gets too close
the croc will hypnotize and lure the bird to open jaws.
Just like in the cartoon. Bad luck to birds.

And bleary-eyed fish. At the aquarium
we rap hard at the glass to startle
or wake the eel from his bone-filled coral lair.
The heaven of ocean-sea mixes the varieties of color
gliding through timeless time. Now
above the music of the clear pool of creation,
we bend toward the sea lions' sleek black heads,
the image of our flesh in an unnamed world.

In these gardens I feel the precious gift of seeing,

not like when I'm home, where everything's smothered
in absence: my father's shirt unwinding on the clothesline,
a man-shape cut into the grass, my own words
stranded somewhere ahead in time, separate.
But here I see a world known only sometimes in dreams,
where the forest opens to spider monkeys and lemurs
nodding from the green shingles of trees.
They seem to know what I want,
a life that's never stranded in this world or theirs.

WOUND

One night it won't be your friend
stammering at the door for words to say you've died.
Your soul will have already arrived,
a silent star aloft, cold and isolate in the black,
wrung white into grief.
                    In dreams
I'm always late at the hour of savage truth,
crossing dunes and a broken seawall
only to find you, the brother I can't save,
floating face down in the surf.
All at once I'm dawnstruck,
but my eyes see only darkness and you
aglow with moonlight staggering in the yard,
No real speech, numb words mangled,
butchered by the force of some drug or fear
that stretches you tight between two trees.

Then I know I need to find you
in that dim room we shared as children years ago.
Across our ceiling's fractured night sky
I moved my flashlight, a moth-dance
scoring the dark to quiet your first nightmares,
singing words that cannot quiet now
the accumulated sum of years.

Tonight I wait for a word.
I press your hand warmly in mine.
You look at me, try to speak
the moment a nurse glides in
packing with more gauze your throat

slashed by a punk's switchblade.
The miserable room fills with unknowing...
We must have lived to know this pause.

THIS WORLD ELSEWHERE

PILSEN (CHICAGO)

1.

When rain comes she smells fire
and stands by the window, visible
to herself in the field of lights.
She sees it spread in pools
on the wallpaper, no chance
for her children to swim away
across the surf. Outside
the rain turns to sleet scouring
black brickface tenement walls.

Once, as a girl, she took the bus
alone from Blue Island to Cicero,
and spent the day with her cousin.
A backyard of iris and daisies,
bees nipping sunflowers, a cat
asleep on the dog-eared fence,
the smell of wildwood on her lips.
On the ride home, a man asked
to share her place, then touched her.

Aglow inside her nightdress,
she stands on the fire escape,
watching the El stream past,
each window like a picture frame,
curious faces smeared and crushed
by forgetfulness, unknowing.
If she dared become what she sees
she'd know the pictures are words
containing other words, a life
dreamed elsewhere, yet here.

2.

He dresses all in black because
black's the color of death,
and death's what he unwinds
from fists like squalls of rage.
He writes on walls,
Nación de Guerrilleros & Sencillo Carnicería
When he drives at night on Cullerton,
he tells the others with him
to shoot the first man or third woman
that turns the corner at 23rd,
then loads the rifle in his lap,
glancing once at the fullmoon overhead . . .

Morning light warms his face.
He sits outside his mother's back door
hearing the racket inside begin:
chairs scraping, children crying,
his mother's raspy cough,
toilet and cracked basin.
He hates the way it sounds
of earth-song crying to water.
He doesn't need memory,
only his hands and these streets
swelling with panic and blood-song.
A breath whispers and grunts
behind his ear. He doesn't know
how short his life is going to be.

BANNERS

(El Monte,

California:

1933)

For

Luis

Arroyo

ur men drank water and never smoked
as they sat under the walnut tree,
green branches enfolding them,
green leaves flaming with sunlight.
They came each day as dawn approached,
tense dark men crowding together
and speaking low in the presence
of the morning star. We women
could hear the winds shifting south
over the empty fields.
                              Hours passed.
Our children chewed sticks
like ears of corn, dust-devils
whirled and dissolved in the road.
At noon the sheriffs passed
in steaming black cars.
Nothing looked changed: the same
huddled shacks below the sun,
a yellow dog rising from a gully,
dungarees on a sagging clothesline.
So they passed on, riding out
the horizon as our singers
plucked a noisy chord.
                              When they emerged
stiff, morose, the evening rattle
had already begun in the trees.
Tomorrow we'll march to the fields, they said.
We brought them a sip of coffee
cooled by the breath of the night wind
and watched their faces screw up

25

as they said goodnight and turned homeward
over fields brimming with fruit.

: : :

In a week the strikebreakers came.
Another week and the sheriffs
lured our men into the station
with lies, promises of good work.
And the Mexican consul there
sporting a pencil-stick moustache,
a solemn porky bastard who
sprouted among our dazzled men
calling them "reds." After that
we kept up the daily pickets
and mass meetings and prayers.

The first time we drove our trucks
through town, forty women maybe,
shouting, making the place a bee hive,
raw sunburnt faces stared at us
on every street. That was all right.
But one man, alone, swore at us.
Bracing his hips by the roadside,
hard blue eyes burning right through us,
he wished us bloodied and raped.
I never knew why the town existed,
but now I knew what I felt,
and that was my own heart staring
at itself, blood running not singing.

Returning at twilight, I stared
at the dark fields slipping past us,
the air hot and always doubled,
smell of youngberries rotting . . .
Now I could no longer find hope

because we buried three small children
and put the sticks they chewed
upon that ground, one on each grave,
there in the summer harvest light.

: : :

I can still see those nameless stars
poking through the roof slats at night,
green and blue and plum-colored stars.
Eyes shut, I watched them holding still
while I rolled past them on a wave
as if the whole night were an ocean sea.
I never dreamed of food. That night
I woke at the sound of a small
tapping on the roof, the room cool
spread out around me like a wood.
My husband slept, his fine tangled head
on my arm, mouthing words that have
always stayed with me: *ya 'cabaron todo,
the sticks an' all.*
                    The hour comes back
in the dust thick with panicked men.
Harsh cries sang out from the workers
throwing their heads behind them,
a lightning flash through yellow clouds.
Three were blasted, rolling into
a ditch where they lay face down
licking the mossy earth. Some of us
were pulled away screaming, *Murderers!
Brothers!* Then we scattered
like nightmare leaves over the valley.
In a windless orchard we began to weep.

PAPA CAYO

Arriero from my village, north of here,
I come with my two good burros,
sure-footed and gentle, descending
the volcano to the rocky plain below,
tin pans, ladles, cups, and hand mirrors,
all packed tightly in bundles that shake
like the humps of camels side to side.

In Tierra Caliente, it is always summer
as I arrive among the Indians who take me in.
They remind me of my children at home,
trusting but smarter than me; they speak like birds.
And I, with my beardless face and slant eyes,
speaking coarse Spanish, could be their cousin
or long lost brother come home.

We have a drink they make from some
local tree. It is sweet and cool
(after days through mountain passes
and scrub hills) like dark shining well water.
Perhaps it is their water
scooped from flowers flared like horns.
Perhaps that's why their voices sing.

I spend days at first listening to their elders
who talk of such things as the end of the world.
And when I see the stars at night
exploding into darkness, I believe.
The one called Josiah sits stoking the fire,
feeling his way to the end of his words,

the fire seeds he tosses searing the air.

Nights pass, and what's here spreads patiently
each morning: forests mixed with fog,
dawnlight yawning over thatched roofs,
globes of ovens smoking with green wood.
My goods spread on the ground are poor handworks
beside the gifts they bring out for me, among them
a white conch shell from the sea no one remembers.

Before the rains come I turn homeward.
Tall veering arcs of rain, they tell me,
rainbows of rain filling the sky,
pouring freely over the village,
over the village and then the world.
I have seen it only in my dreams,
but it is the same, the same.

We say goodbye. Each time
I have to think not to hug these people
but stretch my hand and say *Luck* or *God bless*.
And each time they reach out,
and with one shy finger calmly touch
the palm of my open hand
as if the soul were nestled there.

LUMINARIAS

THREE

FOR A KICKAPOO GIRL

Go stand in the rain, then.
Clouds are rising early tonight
and you could not do without the moon.

Moon Woman peers over the stars.
Are you singing, dancing now?
Will you wear sage at dawn?

I would like to know
how the rain takes your dress,
how it gathers your thighs
like the hills in Wathena.

I would like to know
how your skin rivers the night,
flowing to the far sea
under a golden sky.

I would like to know
what wind your name unravels on,
and follow it till I am
feathered as a bird in your sight.

THE EARTH

She scooped a handful of shiny pebbles
    From the riverbed, held them
    A long time to her face,
A morning of clear light all around us.
The river stopped, the far hills glowed,
    And from where we knelt
    On the gritty bank
The soft summer air moved on us.
She took care for the smallest things:
    Remembering to touch
    The unmoved stones, to breathe
With her body the whole expanse of light.
All day I dreamed the earth was rising
    From bedrock, from alluvium,
To the wind's slow motion,
    A dance taking ages to perform.

FLINT HILLS

Across the dried, burnt wheat fields of Kansas,
blue herons skimmed close to the shaggy grasstops
looking for a spark of sky, distant morning's shower,
that stirred the crackling plains into old new song.
Clouds rolled back on the warp horizon and blazed,
the cottonwoods nodded, waiting for more rain,
and those sleek gray birds, sovereign messengers,
circled past, slowly, hands waving goodbye.

We drove through the late August heat toward evening,
the land changing itself almost impudently
to a tide of low hills that held flinty earth compact.
"The Indians carved serpents into the buffalo grass
and grass roots," you read from your book,
"here where the wind endstops." That was ages ago.
Your voice kept my eye falling down across the hills,
the calm valleys in between dark with shadow.

Past Strong City, you snapped your book shut
and squinted through the windshield at the first stars.
Naming them, before the great pale light had turned
to a sensuous dark of galaxies, of nebulae,
you knew how forced that was, and fell silent,
contenting yourself now with the wind
that blew cool, warm, for miles,
repeating the song of light freed from earth.

For me, seeing your land for the first time,
the visit was swallowed whole by summer's untimely end,
by the stories of the land I tried to dream up,
stories no one can possibly see
in the wash of starlight on hard blacktop.
I mumbled that there were still trains to Kansas City
and that thought was swallowed too
as the shadow of the arena rose in the west.

Music blared from the wall of the bleachers topped
by a halo of shooting floodlights. We locked arms,
maneuvering through the scrambled lot of pickups,
station wagons, old battered sedans and jeeps,
headlights and dust raking the ground,
the only clear image in a wilderness of noise.
Then through the lines already swelling at the gate,
filling the stands inside with their prairie dream-voices.

Spinning beyond the lights into dazzling shapes
the pageant of flags entered the oval field,
men and women racing on horseback,
crisscrossing rapidly, flawlessly,
lengths and lengths of color pulled by our eyes.
They sliced through the air like gulls or geese,
till finally a lone man-at-arms gestured
and all the lines stopped at once.

Leaving the oval field at the far gate,
the riders waved to the hoots of the crowd.
We looked down into the fading afterimage
as clowns and bellowing steers absorbed the scene.
There were other scenes, and midway,
a brief rustle of kids and critters.
Always the crowd, the lights, the stars above,
figures and forms innumerable and unnamed.

We left the arena, hoping to see the hills alone.
Others stood outside in the lot, silent,
dreaming on the stars, the night that gives nothing
but what we ask: faint stars on which to dream,
a voice of unimpoverished desire at our interior.
You threw your hands upon my downcast face
then gave me back my own lost look. The wet
parched grass spread tracers of light at our feet.

WALKING

I imagine what can never happen:
the valley of Oaxaca stretching away at dawn,
its black volcanoes topped with snow,
an angle of birds in flight,
and we together, in love, walking
beneath an ocean of clouds.

for P.F.

And now I find, half-buried in the glazed sand,
a woman's sandals, ancient, beautiful.
You bend near, touching where the wind
has blown clear the silence,
straps, hemp strings, red woven bands,
and years, waiting in that silence.
I lift them to the sunlight,
and something in the distance pulls you away,
leaving me here, alone, watching
the soles of your feet on the bright waves.

How like you to move toward the distance,
crossing every border that you find.
How unlike me to wait for you,
calling the air between us to bring you back.
I don't know why you don't hold me close
and can't let me go. But in your time
of movement and light you make the silence
of my soul a time in which I'm saved.
The way you change changes me.
What I find you've already scattered to the wind.

Yes, I imagine what will never happen.
But what I imagine assumes a world
where the pale blue air is your signature,
a life just beyond your eyes' pursuit,
a world where the light renews my eyes
and makes my hands accurate and keen.
Between earth and sky you go walking,
my airy girl, my discipline,
taking on light, the color of waves,
real life I've only just now entered.

LUMINARIAS

The bus ride at evening, mother,
that showers the beet field
with a small snow, then dust,
consoles me as much as your heart
now that you've come back from
the shadows of three days' sleep
where you might have stayed,
picking clean the harvest of your youth.
You've come back. And now that
I'm returning, too, the obscure stars
studded in the sky, drop down
and bead the dark with a rich
changeless glow, that I begin
to hear as song, rejoicing in the night.

HOMECOMING

To the city storefronts locked
with black metal gates and iron bars,

to the five a.m. sweeper that slips past
over dirty streets, plastic bags

stuck to light poles ripping overhead in the wind.
This first hour, a false dawn,

as I walk head bowed to the pavement,
snowflakes catching fire in headlights

slicing the air. I'm home, again,
into quiet, lighted waters.

I see not the distance crossed but the shorter
middle ground, a space in and around

my parents' home, vibrating
with some new old message there.

On the porch, I feel the flooring sag
under the weight of years

knocking me off balance,
my keyless hand gripping the icy doorknob.

I stand awash in the morning's ghostly light
till I see my mother's shape moving

behind the glass, descending the stair
like I've seen a thousand times from inside.

Now outside, it saves me from the fall
into eternal wintry dark.

She opens the door, her arms,
a warm sweep of air behind her.

I hug her small shoulders, patting
the sweat-damp nape of her neck.

"I rode all night to see you."
She pulls at my long hair and turns,

quietly stepping into the dark of the house.
"Your father had a feeling you might come."

Lighting the stove, she's lit by pale flames,
her face a photograph of something past

but not forgotten, her words
a song pulling me out of the shadows.

And in our sight we recognize each other,
as if for the first time,

mother and son, unknown lovers,
repeating mysteries of faith.

PACIFICA

FOUR

PACIFICA

On the pier below the lightless mountains
they lean into the winds blown from night,
the dark Pacific swell sprinkled with seabirds.
Land's end, in late summer, cold here,
a rocky coast gouged by winter storms
massing like armies out at sea.
Gathering their tackle in silent pairs
the fishermen begin the long trek back to their cars,
amber figures in the glow of overhead mercury lamps.
Inland, across the coastal road,
the sandy luminous shoulder blows drifts
around the night. This nocturnal world
of seacliffs gorged with clay,
and tinny voices rising above the surf,
what has it to do with memory and change?
Yes, it's a lonely kingdom.
The salty air it sends (from some great
obscure existence) is potent sorrow.
Rocks, palms, hillside homes,
all weathered and resigned to a declining sleep.
But the heavenworks sing madly,
a maze of circles and squares drawn ever higher,
as far up as, who can say?
I know it's no real part of me,
a stranger here, trying to see everything
as if it all must somehow matter.
From the pier the last to leave are gaping
at countless stars, fishlines going slack,
then taut, over and over.
They draw traps spilling white on white,

and small, barnacled hungry crabs
struggle in cages looped with greasy kelp.
Something at the sea's source
pulls back from down there.

A RAINY DAWN

rainy dawn now
       slants seaward, bringing
            a few leaves,
earthly strays,
       that sweep past the window
          in perfect silence.
I wake to that motion
       as if tossed there too,
          a cast-out papery heart
loosed in seabound wind.
       Dreams, wind, waves,
          the mournful turning
of uncertain promise
       I've lived through
          again, this day.
I've lost the word
       I wanted to say . . .
          and the question begins.

AT TWILIGHT

At twilight the churchbells beat slowly
(now you're lying beside me).

All things fade into the past,
even your green eyes

which just now closed against
that unspeakable sound of love.

I stand in this room,
a shadow against the wall,

waiting to hear the sound a second time
(now I'm fading in the dark).

POEM

I saw your absence and, gazing on,
felt the wind brush my downcast face
like an odd, gently pitying hand.
In pools of winter rain and bracken,
I saw you reflected there,
a silvery image breaking all apart
as the wind lifted and you whistled an odd song
that found its way into my bloodless heart.
O I wanted to turn, turn,
and lose that instant of potent loss,
your smiling face unpooling before my eyes,
but like a tree wrapped in winter I was caught.
I raised my head, your eyes flashed green,
desperate from the flood that broke above us in waves.

JUNE LETTER

The outdoors fill again with voices,
fill around you, as now you walk
the old delta town you love,
three hours' daylight ordering the streets—
and my voice, perhaps, there too.
I wish for that, still in bed,
then long after as I keep to this quiet place,
light a dwelling that loosens
all speech at the bottom of grief.

Last night, from our room,
I watched the neighbors gather
inside a livingroom window.
There they were, all together,
goldstain of candlelight drenching them.
Then music, deep voices,
blew through the night
a golden anguish of prayer.
We heard that singing once before.
We were safely rooted then.
But now alone, listening,
watching our bedroom ceiling
where light spilled upward
against the dark, I wished to be
only what that song was,
to have my empty arms full
of your sleeping, your happiness.

No love or grace or sign
comes from nowhere, but always late.
Your photo gleams on the nightstand
burdened with afternoon light.
How many days ago did you take that smile
which takes from me all I never knew I had?
I finger your things: tin owl,
parasols, seaweed crape, and feathers.
The wind enters through the open door,
the fluent hands of absence lofting this page.
If absence is the only thing I know,
how long will it take to fill with words
until you emerge, complete?
I love you more than my words.
I love you more, and that, too, emerges
in this summer light.

DREAMING

Sometimes it's mere story, full enough,
life choosing its own moments to recall.
A fox pounces on a stump
in a golden field. Spilling light
a fountain gurgles with song.
But even dreaming this I know
that any fable or gross unbidden fact
is a division sustained at dawn.

I wake by stars in scattered flight.
Earth and sky, one blue abyss
to cross with open eyes measuring
the moon's empty track, lovely,
but by degrees released from sight.
Then your dream-voice calls from a heap of dark
and I'm surrounded by great slabs
of stunned, silent air, forcing me down

past rooms and corridors in deep brilliance,
until I'm standing on the infinite
covered space of earth. To all your words
—telling me now what I believe—
I can neither weep nor close my eyes
and unsay what's left of you,
what you've become, in passing from me
to this impossible dream of day beginning.

OLEANDER

On chill Pacific mornings
they seem unreal,
edging the suburbs
in green lastingness
with pink and ivory blossoms
like I never saw
in my old city.
I turn my head and go.
But they're so much with me,
jostling in fog,
strangling a fence,
massing at the sea
or walking up from it.
In darkness they sweep
the wall outside my room
till everything seems
thinned out
and the moon
about to break in.

I wonder if that sound
is their voices,
the real sound
calling to me,
calling me to the world
I scarcely know?
Could their voices be
redolent of love?
Then why the fear,
the ache,

of inhaling too deeply
the sound of
that love,
as if one's own death
waited inside
the oiled casks of those buds?

I knew a girl once
who took a handful,
smiling at me *(Smell?),*
and buried her face in those blooms.
Then, eyes shut,
the approaching secret
stopping the smile,
Oleander! spilled
from her stupefied lips
Are poison.
I took her home,
and as she lay in bed
something was withheld,
something other than love,
that from the flowers
of her eyes
broke out
and brushed the shadowy
air between us.
She pulled a pillow over her face
and sobbed long
and hard into it,
muffling the secret
I only learned
by measures.

At night I walk
along these streets,
refusing the glow
of households,
the rank presence
of a man or woman
in the silken fluency of
bedroom or corridor.
Instead I want
the rain
to break and break on me,
wetting the pines
and eucalyptus trees,
the black oleanders,
blooms
spread all around,
the deepest
luminescence.

PARIS

FIVE

BOULEVARD DE SEBASTOPOL

Past the boutiques, cafés, and banks,
the crowds go moving in both directions,
feet scraping the old flagstones
while the sound of traffic erases thought.
The March air is cold and gray here,
a flurry of snow, heavy ground,
the accumulated months of darkness
not yet ready to burst this tedium of
atonement. I think of the long trip home,
but I'm still in my old familiar city,
an unseen pinpoint in the spectral dark.
From here, I see myself there,
fingering a few coins in my pocket
as I cross into the rich, noisy flow.

The Gypsy children, alert to the ignorance
of tourists and strangers like myself,
pick their way through the crowd
hoping for one lucky haul.
Spite and savvy are all they have.
They need shoes and could stand a bath.
I've seen their men sprawled on sidewalks,
a blank cardboard sign in their hands.
They don't see me drop a few coins,
only stare at the stonegray city.
Who knows where they come from?
Not this place, which doesn't see them,
only hears the chaos of their tongues
as when they surrounded me, the elected.

A girl, sixteen maybe, a shepherdess,
wrapped in a brown tattered shawl of wool,
her eyes red bark and wet slate stone,
held up a baby's sick and swollen face,
thrust it in my face, screaming,
"Pour le baby! Pour le baby!"
the shining eyes like pebbly slime
staring back at me, ironic and cruel.
Then I felt one of her small hands
try to slip inside my pocket
as she cried and cried. I jerked back,
and saw no one taking notice of us.
The world kept pushing along
the boulevard, unchanged, resolved,

resolving into a million graystone blocks
that struck me with flat, dumb amazement.
The want of love beggared me.
I looked into her eyes, the world there
disappearing from sight,
and all I had thought real and certain
was taken from me by her brute look.
When it was done, it tossed me
like a rag back onto the street.
I gave her some coins, not for her,
not for all the wronged or despairing like her,
but for forgiveness sake,
the last ruined gift. Wordlessly,
she turned and vanished into the crowd.

And I stayed there on the sidewalk,
poised before the subway entrance,
a long sharp drop into darkness.
I didn't want to go down inside
because she was leaving forever,
and I couldn't get rid of that thought.

Then for a moment, the perfect unreal
infant face flashed in the wintry air,
and stared at me now in strange
astonishment and displeasure.
It quickly fled, like passion,
as if snatched away by doubt,
leaving behind the clear sound of traffic
ringing in an inexpressible emptiness.

ON PONT MARIE

for

Paul

Celan

Time beyond the horizon
is the only thing you follow,
that lures you on. And there
in the shuddering cold
which is the past, I stand
looking over the Seine's icy landing.
You were here, and went.
I feel your passing, bleak angel.
The sky is ashen where you
hurled yourself up,
out of horror and pity,
into inaudible breathing.
And the only sound that comes down
is a vague scrim of falling snow.
It comes down no real shadow
on me, and yet I feel
its fearful touch.

To eat of bread you touched,
to taste those fiery waves,
changes the feel of time.
Will you come back for us,
out of bitter wind and rain,
tense with explanations?
Your heat would melt these stones
and fire the day's events,
torch us in bad sleep.
Night comes where the river ends.
The water's glazed light
twitters into memory.

I'm stuck here, watching
the clotted traffic, a monster
belching noise and eating streets.
It is always already too late
to save you or be saved.

NOTRE DAME

A batwing shadow blips the stained glass light.
The saints looking down see only us
standing beside the wrought iron balustrade:
tourists, schoolchildren, burnt-out believers,
gazing toward the voluptuous forms and colors
that shine their steady light on our unfinished time.
No worship here, only a century's dire need
to restore that luminous mystery to suffering flesh.
I hear the guide's voice move farther off
into the cathedral's bones, a mere echo now
as I wander alone to the other side.
                                        Before me,
as if I'd crossed miles of freezing air, I see
the Virgin of Guadalupe in a dark niche
large enough to show they cared to honor her.
A single small light shines on her tremblingly .
The Virgin's face, turned slightly away, smiling
down on the peasant's kneeling ghost, is still lustrous
though cracked by stress of wars and all heart's ache.
Men and women, our hands and time fallen,
falling apart in the wind. Here in church
I feel released into that vision of dispersal.

Two women cross themselves in the old way,
and I hear that muttering sound at my back,
housed in another church twenty years distant
where I'd kneel staring long and hard at the altar
until it exploded in a golden light and stung my eyes,
returning me to a December's quiet morning mass.
But I see no version of myself here,

no signs of a history acted out before, in need.
And I know my hunched, darkened form
won't be found in the Indian mother's plaster eyes—
a miniature drawing, identical life.

The tour heads this way, aiming cameras everywhere.
Someone snaps my picture. And I laugh to think
I'm stuck there, a lesser portrait in that colder eye.
What would Juan Diego say? *Lo siento mucho,* perhaps.
But disordered saints who imagine they love the goddess
make no sound after a lifetime rendering themselves
and all things in their power to heaven's will.
The heavenward mind, seeing the divine's nearness
in the stars, wants other knowledge than what we have
here where our votives light our presence
through the dark. I turn and leave the way I came.

In the gift shop I buy a rosary, read some prayer.
Outside the pigeons burst in dizzy flight
wing to wing like so many leaves lifted into air.
But there are no leaves. The trees and windows,
all muted this time of year, stand apart among the birds
that suddenly darken the gracenotes of morning light.
The future comes to mind like a thought that's past.
In a week a bomb will kill passengers on a train
traveling second class from Lyon. Which of them
will see angels or the bright lady's grieving face?
Or see real bats flying in caverns of salt and rock?

LA PLACE DES AFRICAINS

The metro spills passengers curbside
where no one but me pitches his face
to the cold March rain. It falls tonight
silent and calm on my foreign city.
I'm in one vast city all my life,
climbing steps or walking streets,
faulted and shaky wherever I go.
It's no way home, but I
only want to feel my way, just that,
until I feel borrowed by the world.
I listen to the rain's voice
carve its ignorance into my flesh
and look heavenward as the Eiffel Tower
rises immense in the smoldering floodlights.

It stands like a god or black scaffolding
to the god I've never seen,
but whose silent touch, like rain,
is everywhere too much tonight.
The citybound dark thins out.
The drenched shadows of men appear.
Isolate in the square, the Africans stand around
blankets spread on the flagstone ground—
jewelry, watches, key chains, lighters,
beaded in the silvery rain.
They try to snag the wandering tourists
who pause and look, but won't buy.
Deux cents francs! Look at this!
they holler for common junkwares,

and every word from their lips
dies in a cloud of cold night air
where song may once have been.
I pause too, squatting and staring
at two figures, elephant idols,
carved from ebony timbers that rise
in some distant rain forest, hauled here
with ores and gems and other loot,
trailing voices along the way.
It's an old world I can't really see
only feel its massive loss
in these twin silent shapes
that hold me in their gaze,
until I feel unmade in time,

like the worshipper entering the dark
through the silence of the forest.
My mind roughs out a black lake
where I hear its bottomless voice,
a voice that speaks without words
as in a dream. This space I exist in
breaks the need to storm the world,
and my heart catches at the thought.
At my back, the god's voice:
Not too much. Not too much today.
I'm smiling up at the tall shade,
as the floodlights explode behind him,
the icy spring rain melting
in the sumptuous chaos of my eyes.

AN UNWRITTEN LETTER

From the train, no dawn scorching the field.
Everywhere rain pools black and weighs
down upon solitary trees. Miles
through dark, changeless lowlands, I watch
the rain pushing along the window,
no earth outside, no distance,
only the afterimage of the station crowd,
fading shadows on the platform.
There was one so close I could see
her blue-shell necklace stippling the dark,
iridescent with fine wavering lines.
The woman's image mocked my desire.
She wasn't you whose love, like anger,
hates desire whipped up in absence.
She looked deep into the huge spattered glass
behind which I sat, visible to myself,
as the train slipped forward slowly
and pulled into the long smokeblack tunnel.
I stared ahead toward us now,
in our dark room of pure memory,
where we press our contrary needs
against faint, obliging wants.
I see stellar darkness, not what I know.
And you, inhabiting your body's coiled light,
alone, not worldless, but apart,
breathe worlds away from what I want.
Now that dark turns all wintry white
like a new soft-fallen page of snow,
and I'm gazing on the unscribbled ledger
of a life that's hardly known.

Yet I feel the future as something past,
lived out, finished, before it's born.
Dawn rises where a black lake appears.
Suddenly I'm awakened by your shade
that cuts across mine in the empty glass.
It shimmers away, bodiless,
and I can't follow, can't weep,
pressed by nameless powerful strangers,
only watch a dark world streaming with rain,
trees bent by earth's thought sinking.

NIGHT SONG

SIX

THREE POEMS IN WINTER

1.

Tonight, caught in a sudden downpour
that announces fall's new remembering,
I watch you drink the night, your heart
an importunate moth fluttering at my side.
Then I see the green oaks ripple,
the rain's long and silvery stream
spread round us here as promise recalled,
and words finally tumble, moth fed, for you.
This warm edge brightens, now binds,
like the circle I've made, ring on ring
of my own silent asking. Tentative now
your eyes take mine into their nets
of dazzle and mist, as you whisper
to my waking dream its own quiet breathing.

2.

In this green watery field, love,
I see everything I'm given to see:
your cantering dream ponies, pale
twilight, and a dark-haired girl
who makes her way toward these, singing.
The wind catches live oaks tossing leaves
around her head. The winter rain pools too
close her in their silvery chimes.
To hold this vision all through winter—
when rainstorms and cold fires lengthen endlessly
in a day, a year, an hour—
that's what I live for, here, today,
one bright greening world
made visible in this local light.

3.

At first light, before we sleep,
we see the flowers in the garden
through the open box window,
claiming our bed with new dampness.
For a moment we're exactly what we see:
the starry flowers, flowery stars,
rooted in a terrestrial sky
that brightens, fades, with early light.
In this impossible moment, awake forever,
there's no distance, no frontier,
no sweet watery fields to cross
with believing, beautiful dreams,
only ourselves, the silence of one bed,
which is enough for us to learn.

Como las tinieblas en mi soledad, cae el rocío en campo verde
y mi corazón brinca de gozo. A lo lejos en la distancia
oigo una tierna voz que me dice: "Has llegada a tu destino."
                    —Candelaria Estrada de Rodríguez

Last night was clear and cold,
the face of the earth perfectly still,
as if the day would never arrive
to bear witness to your snowy
Christlike anguish.

I set down your own words here
in this desolation of certainty,
wakeful in the solar light that breaks
and receives your beautiful language
and touches my grief.

TO MY MOTHER

The new year's about to fall,
and all through the neighborhood
it's summer in winter.
The air shines all around,
the maples look studded.
Oh that they might bloom,
bloom and be the news of life in death
if these final merciful days
could stretch on, undiminished.

We sit the same on the porch in silence,
watching children fly along the street
trailing Christmas wrappings.
Your eyes, watery and almost blue,
follow them toward your future
beyond the sun-glazed street, beyond the trees,
to the sea so far beyond our porch.

Seven winters have sucked your life,
now a suffering thing.
I'd give you mine, mother,
but while you suffer I'm dying to myself,
the child you'll leave behind,
his best hope unmade or betrayed
a second time. The years
darken and fall in you.

Or will my heart be renewed?
You'll leave behind this question too
and one of your gestures,
as now you turn toward me, smiling,
and wave at the boys and girls
running into the light,
your arm a splint of palm
wrapped in gauze. That gesture—
and it's one I've never seen,
the turn and look, too, undreamed of—
makes me wish to match the spirit
by which you call to those children
aglow like blossoms beyond the bare trees.

NIGHTSONG

Their voices storm the poplars and cottonwoods
bare and needlelike in the fullmoon light.
I don't know what they're saying,
only watch the great man-sized fire burning,
bud-shaped stars overhead. The elder
sings fiercely to the harvest moon,
the voices behind him rolling on themselves,
then tosses a handful of light into the flames.
A brief smell, sweet, fills the air.
Our quiet breathing takes its place.

The drumbeat source, heart of the night,
rising and falling like no familiar stuff,
can't be caught or guessed as it goes,
though night voices repeat that sound
bonded of dreams and heaven's compassing light.
There's a door beyond this moment,
then woods in snow, a wide insurgent sky,
hawks gliding past the river and hills
where we all emerge on a frozen band of dawn,
bright particles tossed away by heart.